I Can Work!

Sharon Coan, M.S.Ed.

I work.

I get a work **chart**.

My Work Chart
Devan
Jobs
My Stars
feed dog
make bed
dishes
clean room
SOAP

I feed Sam.

My Work Chart
Devan
Jobs
My Stars
feed dog
make bed
dishes
clean room

I get a star.

My Work Chart
Devan
Jobs
My Stars
feed dog
make bed
dishes
clean room
SOAP

I make my bed.

My Work Chart
Devan
Jobs
My Stars
feed dog
make bed
dishes
clean room

I get a star.

I help Mom.

My Work Chart
Devan
Jobs
My Stars
feed dog
make bed
dishes
clean room

I get a star.

I feel **proud**!

Chart It!

1. Get your supplies.
2. Make a work chart.

3. Do some work.

4. Add stars.

Glossary

chart—a list

proud—to feel happy about something you have done well

work—to do a job

Index

Your Turn!

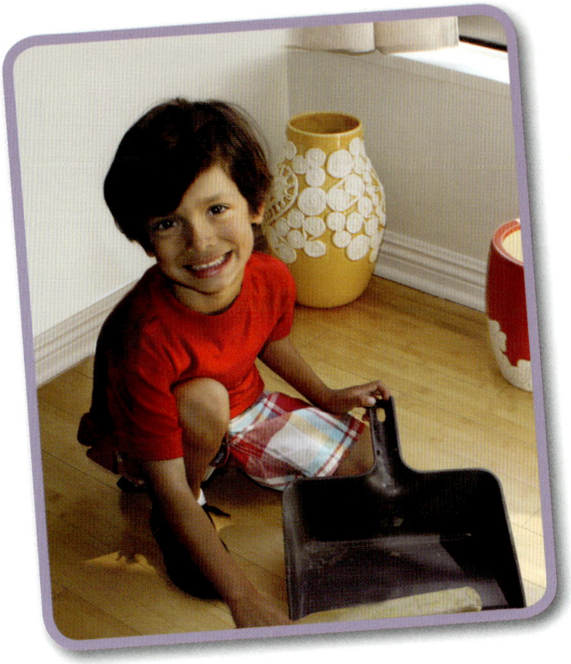

What work do you do at home? Draw a picture.

My Work Chart
Devan
Jobs
My Stars
feed dog
make bed
dishes
clean room

Consultants

Shelley Scudder
Gifted Teacher
Broward County Schools

Caryn Williams, M.S.Ed.
Madison County Schools
Huntsville, AL

Publishing Credits

Conni Medina, M.A.Ed., *Managing Editor*
Lee Aucoin, *Creative Director*
Torrey Maloof, *Editor*
Lexa Hoang, *Designer*
Stephanie Reid, *Photo Editor*
Rachelle Cracchiolo, M.S.Ed., *Publisher*

Image Credits: Lexa Hoang.

Teacher Created Materials
5301 Oceanus Drive
Huntington Beach, CA 92649-1030
http://www.tcmpub.com

ISBN 978-1-4333-7350-3

Printed in Malaysia
THU001.48806